The English Aristocracy:
A Beginner's Guide to Their Titles, Rank, and Forms of Address

J. Robinson

www.firestonebooks.com

The English Aristocracy:
A Beginner's Guide to Their Titles, Rank, and
Forms of Address
J. Robinson

2014 Edition

Published by Firestone Books

ISBN-13: 978-1500465124

www.firestonebooks.com

You can also find out more by following Firestone Books on Facebook and Twitter

Contents

Introduction

The Aristocracy of England, Ireland, Scotland and Wales have, for generations, enjoyed great wealth and great power, and over the centuries have helped forge the political landscape of both Britain and Ireland. Their privileged status was not destined to last however, and their great power has slowly eroded away over the last century and a half, with falling crop prices, inheritance tax, and their gradual loss of political power. But despite their relative decline, the aristocracy, with their rich history and their grand houses, hold a great fascination for many people both in Britain and abroad. Today, tourists flock in ever greater numbers to stately homes, and it seems people still cannot get enough of the many films, books and television shows that are replete with fictional nobility.

This book is not a history of the English aristocracy, nor a book on the aristocratic families of England. It is an introduction to the rules that govern aristocratic titles, answering questions such as: Why might one aristocratic woman be called Lady Jane, another Lady Smith, and another still called the Honourable Jane Smith? Does a duke rank more highly than a marquess? Do the eldest sons of barons rank above the younger sons of earls? If a woman divorces her titled husband, does she keep her title? What if the wife of a viscount is widowed – does she keep her title? Who bestows these titles? Are they still bestowed today? And so on.

Not all eventualities are covered, and some minor exceptions to the many rules have been omitted, but this book is, hopefully, a gentle introduction to the workings of the titles of English nobility. If there is sufficient demand, there may be an updated edition of this book, probably in the far future, giving greater detail regarding aristocratic titles and their usage.

This book covers peers, baronets and knights. It is true that many modern knights, have achieved their titles through services to sport, entertainment, and so on, and would not see themselves as aristocrats. However, given the strong historic links between knights and the aristocracy, information on knights has been included in this book.

This book does not cover royalty, nor does it cover Scottish barons, the High Kingship of Ireland and other titles that are specific to the Celtic nations, though time-to-time these titles may be mentioned where relevant, given the intertwined histories of England, Scotland, Wales and Ireland. It may be that in the future, Celtic Nobility, British Royalty and other titled people are covered either in an updated version of this book, or in separate volumes.

There are also portions of writing that stray slightly

from the English aristocracy, for instance the chapters on Lords of the Manor and on the Landed Gentry. These chapters and other segments are included given their close relationship the aristocracy of England, and the other members of the upper classes.

Some of the peerages given in this book are fictional (usually when giving generic examples, such as in the chapters on forms of address) and some in the book are real (usually when specific examples are needed).

This book contains some repetition between chapters, and the author apologises for this. You may read the book from cover to cover, but, if you prefer, it should be possible to dip in and out of the chapters as you wish.

As well as giving information on how to better understand the titles of the English aristocracy, this book also gives information on how to address peers, baronets and knights, as well as a brief histories of the various titles. At the end of the book, there are some appendices which may be of interest to the reader, including some answers to frequently asked questions, some useful contact details, a helpful glossary of terms, information on servants, and information on the order of precedence.

Peers

Introduction to Peers

Members of the peerage are normally addressed by one of five titles which, in descending order, are: duke, marquess, earl, viscount and baron. Peers rank above baronets who, in turn, with a few exceptions, rank above knights.

Peers, historically, were the heads of many of the most powerful families in the country. They had great estates, and derived much of the wealth from crops grown on their land, and from the tenants who paid to live there. From the middle-ages, peers also sat in the House of Lords, which was for centuries the most powerful political body in England. From the nineteenth century onwards, however, peers' political power, like their wealth, began a long and slow decline.

In 1999 hereditary peers were no longer allowed to sit in the House of Lords as of right, and today only 92 hereditary peers are allowed to sit in the House of Lords, the rest of the seats there being taken by life peers. (More information on life peers is given later in this book.)

The legitimate children of peers (i.e. those born in wedlock) are all entitled to be called by any number of different titles (called courtesy titles) depending on the noble rank of their parents. Younger sons of dukes, for instance, are formally given the title Lord. This, however, has never entitled them to sit in the House of Lords.

Until the twenty-first century, the adopted children of peers were not entitled to any sort of courtesy title. Since 2004 however, adopted children have been allowed to use the same courtesy titles as their siblings, though they are not entitled to inherit peerages from their adopting parents.

All peers are entitled to wear coronets on formal occasions. These coronets have different decorations reflecting the rank of the wearer. Many people who are entitled to wear coronets never get coronets made, but have it adorning their coat of arms to signify their rank.

Peerages today are only given to royalty (such as the Duke and Duchess of Cambridge), and those titles that are given to non-royals, such as knighthoods, are given by the monarch, on advice from the Prime Minister and the Honours Committee.

Since 1965, only three non-royal hereditary peerages have been created, all under Margaret Thatcher's government. Two of these peers died without male heirs, thus meaning their titles became extinct. The third person was former Prime Minister, Harold Macmillan, who was made Earl of Stockton. This title is now held by his grandson, Alexander Macmillan,

2nd Earl of Stockton.

This section on peers covers the five ranks of hereditary peers in descending order, and also life peers. This section also contains brief histories of each title, information on how to address different peers and their families, and brief information on the distinguishing features of peers' mantles and coronets.

Dukes and Duchesses

Rank

A duke is the highest rank of the English (and British) peerage, ranking below royalty and certain officials of the crown, but above marquesses, earls, viscounts and barons.

The first duke to be created in England was Edward the Black Prince in 1337.

The most recent dukedom created was for Prince William who, as well as being made Duke of Cambridge, was also given the titles Earl of Strathearn and Baron Carrickfergus, upon his marriage to Katherine Middleton in 2011. The last non-royal to be made a duke was the Duke of Westminster in 1874 (previously he had been the Marquess of Westminster).

A woman who holds the title to a dukedom in her own right, or is the wife of a duke, is normally styled *duchess*. However an exception to this is the current monarch Elizabeth II, who is known as the Duke of Normandy in the Channel Islands, and is known as the Duke of Lancaster in Lancashire.

A duchess in her own right, is a woman who has inherited the title of duchess, rather than having become a duchess through marriage to a duke. It is very rare for a woman to be a duchess in her own right, as titles tend to get passed along male lines.

The husband of a duchess in her own right, is *not* entitled to be called a duke, unless he happens to already be a duke in his own right. If he was called Mr John Smith before his marriage to a duchess, he would continue to be called Mr John Smith after his marriage.

If a duke divorces, his former wife is still entitled to be styled duchess. Often she will use her first name before the title, for instance the wife of the fictional Duke of Buckminster, might style herself as "Sarah, Duchess of Buckminster" to distinguish herself from any possible future duchess, should the duke remarry.

If a duke dies, his surviving wife is still entitled to be called duchess. However this may cause confusion if the heir to the peerage has a wife, who would also be styled duchess. The widowed duchess is therefore referred to either as the Dowager Duchess (a slightly old-fashioned term) or will use her first name before her title as above, for instance "Sarah, Duchess of Buckminster."

Forms of Address

On envelopes, a duke would be addressed as "(His Grace) The Duke of (place-name)", for instance a letter might be addressed to "His Grace, The Duke of Buckminster", or more simply "The Duke of Buckminster".

At the beginning of a letter, a duke would be addressed either as "My Lord Duke" or "Dear Duke".

On meeting a duke, he should be addressed as "Your Grace" or "Duke".

Often a person on familiar terms with a duke would call him by the place-name in his title, rather than his actual name. For instance, The Duke of Buckminster might simply be called Buckminster by his friends.

On envelopes, a duchess would be addressed as "(Her Grace) The Duchess of (place-name)" for instance a letter might be addressed to "Her Grace, The Duchess of Buckminster" or more simply "The Duchess of Buckminster".

At the beginning of a letter, a duchess would be addressed either as "Madam" or "Dear Duchess".

On meeting a duchess, she should be addressed "Your Grace" or "Duchess".

Addressing a royal duke (or duchess) is a slightly different matter, with "Your Royal Highness" and "His Royal Highness" replacing "Your Grace" and "His Grace." Letters would be addressed to "His Royal Highness the Duke of York", "Her Royal Highness the Duchess of Cambridge," and so on.

Coronet and Mantle

A duke's mantle has four rows of ermine on the cape. His coronet is a silver-gilt circlet with eight silver strawberry leaves. The coronet has a cap of crimson velvet topped with a golden tassel, and is turned up with ermine.

The Children of Dukes and Duchesses

If a Duke has more than one title, his eldest son (known as the heir apparent) though not himself an actual peer, may use one of his father's lesser titles 'by courtesy'. If the eldest son of a duke also has an eldest son, then this grandson of a peer may use a still lower title, if one exists.

For example, the Duke of Norfolk is also the Earl of Arundel and the Lord Maltravers. His eldest son, by courtesy, is styled Earl of Arundel, and the Earl of Arundel's eldest son, if he had one, would be styled Lord Maltravers. However, only the Duke of Norfolk is actually a peer; his son, the Earl of Arundel, and his grandson Lord Maltravers, despite their courtesy titles, remain commoners. (Also, legally, though his son and grandson may be called by the titles mentioned, the Duke of Norfolk still holds *all* the titles.)

Courtesy peerages are only used by the peer's eldest living son, and the eldest son's eldest living son, and so on.

The wives of courtesy peers are also entitled to courtesy titles, which are the female equivalents of their husbands' titles, so the wife of the Earl of Arundel would be styled Countess of Arundel. Also, the children of the Earl and Countess of Arundel would be entitled to use the same courtesy titles as the children of someone who is an Earl in his own right (see the section on Earls and Countesses for more information).

The actual courtesy title which is given to the eldest son of a duke is a matter of family tradition. For instance, the eldest son of the Duke of Buccleugh is styled Earl of Dalkeith, even though the duke is also Marquess of Dumfriesshire, a title which outranks an earldom.

If a duke does not have any subsidiary titles his eldest son may use the courtesy title of "Lord (Surname)". This differs slightly from the title given to younger sons.

Another form of courtesy title is the honorific prefix of "(The) Lord" before the name, for instance The Lord John Smith. This non-peerage title is accorded to younger sons of dukes. It does not, and has never, entitled the holder to sit in the House of Lords. The title may continue to be used after the death of the holder's father, but this courtesy title does not enable the children of Lords by courtesy to have titles of their own.

The wife of someone with a courtesy title is entitled to the feminine form of her husband's title, which takes the form of "(The) Lady", followed by her husband's name, for example Lady John Smith. The fairly rare exception to this is if the wife herself is the daughter of a duke, marquess or earl, in which case she would keep her own courtesy title. For instance, if Lady Emma Pargetter, daughter of an earl, should marry Lord John Smith, the younger son of a duke, she would now be known as Lady Emma Smith – not Lady John Smith.

The younger son of a duke, and holder of the courtesy title "Lord", may be addressed orally as "Lord John" or "My lord". If he has a wife, she would be addressed orally as "Lady John" or "My lady".

In letters, the younger son of a duke would be addressed "My Lord" or "Dear Lord John", and his wife would be addressed "Madam" or "Dear Lady John".

The honorific prefix of "(The) Lady" is used for the daughters of dukes. The courtesy title is added before the person's given name, so if Jane Smith is the daughter of a duke, she may either be called The Lady Jane Smith, Lady Jane Smith, or Lady Jane (but not Lady Smith).

The title of Lady may still be used after the death of her father but it is not inherited by her children. If Lady Jane Smith married Mr James Fairfax, her husband would not gain any title by virtue of his marriage. Jane would however now be addressed as Lady Jane Fairfax.

Any woman who marries a peer uses the feminine version of his peerage title, even if her father's title is higher than that of her husband, so should Lady Jane

Smith, the daughter of a duke, marry Viscount Washington, she would become Viscountess Washington. This means that as a result of her marriage, she may drop down the order of precedence. (See Appendix D: Order of Precedence.)

In the case of a divorce, the former wife of a titled person may keep the title she acquired upon marriage, if she so wishes. So for instance, if Lord John Smith, the son of a duke, should marry more than once, there can be multiple Lady John Smiths.

Example

Let us say you were invited to the fiftieth birthday of the Duchess of Buckminster and you accepted her invitation. When replying, you might address the envelope to "Her Grace, The Duchess of Buckminster"*, and could choose to begin the letter of acceptance with "Dear Duchess". (Remember this is just one way of addressing her.)

At the party, you might find yourself introduced to her and her husband. You would normally greet the Duchess as "Your Grace", or "Duchess" and her husband as "Your Grace" or "Duke". If other close friends came to speak to the duke, you might well hear them call him Buckminster.

If you met their daughter, Louisa, you might address her as "Lady Louisa." However, as a younger person, she might feel more comfortable for her courtesy title of "Lady" to be dropped, and prefer to just be called Louisa.

Note that The Duke and Duchess of Buckminster are fictional titles.

You may even discretely try and find out in advance how Lady Louisa likes to be addressed, to save any (very slight) embarrassment. It may even be wise to also find out how the Duke and Duchess prefer being greeted beforehand.

Marquesses and Marchionesses

Rank

A marquess ranks above an earl but below a duke. This title comes from the French *marquis* and is sometimes spelled using this French form. Historically a marquess held land called a march. This land was usually on the borders of a country. The land of a count (or earl) was often called a county, and generally was not on the borders. Because a marquess often had land close to potential enemy territory, while the earl (or count) did not, the title of marquess was ranked higher than that of an earl.

The first marquess to be created was Robert de Vere, who was made Marquess of Dublin in 1385 by Richard II. The last marquessate created was for Rufus Isaacs, who was made Marquess of Reading in 1926. Rufus Isaacs' rise through the aristocracy was meteoric: He was knighted in 1910, made Baron Reading in 1914, Viscount Reading in 1916, the Earl of Reading in 1917, and finally Marquess of Reading. His first wife, Alice Cohen, was made a dame, and his second wife was made a life peer, as Baroness Swanborough.

A woman who either holds the title to a marquisate in her own right, or is the wife of a marquess, is normally styled marchioness.

The husband of a marchioness in her own right, is *not* a marquess, unless he happens to already be a marquess in his own right. If he was called Mr James Jackson before his marriage to a marchioness in her own right, he would continue to be called Mr James Jackson after his marriage.

A marchioness is her own right is very rare, and currently there are none.

If a marquess divorces, his former wife is still entitled to be styled marchioness. Often she will use her first name before the title, for instance "Harriet, Marchioness of Stockbridge" to distinguish herself from any possible future marchioness, should the marquess remarry.

If a marquess dies, his surviving wife is still entitled to be called marchioness. However this may cause confusion if the heir to the peerage has a wife, who would also be styled marchioness. The widowed marchioness is therefore referred to either as the Dowager Marchioness or will use her first name before her title as above, for instance "Harriet, Marchioness of Stockbridge."

Forms of Address

On envelopes, a marquess would be addressed as "(The Most Honourable) the Marquess of (place-name)" for instance a letter might be addressed to "The Most Honourable the Marquess of Stockbridge" or more simply "The Marquess of Stockbridge".

Marquesses by courtesy, and their wives are not entitled to the prefix of "The Most Honourable". (A marquess by courtesy, is someone whose father is not only a duke, but also holds other titles, including that of marquess. The son, who would be the heir apparent, is allowed to use this subsidiary title by courtesy.)

At the beginning of a letter, a marquess would be addressed either as "My Lord Marquess" or "Dear Lord (place-name)" for instance "Dear Lord Stockbridge".

On meeting a marquess, he should be addressed "My lord" or "Your lordship" or "Lord (place-name)".

Often a person on familiar terms with a marquess would call him by the place-name in his title, rather than his actual name. For instance, The Marquess of Stockbridge might simply be called Stockbridge by his friends.

On envelopes, a marchioness would be addressed as

"(The Most Honourable) the Marchioness of (place-name)" for instance a letter might be addressed to "The Most Honourable the Marchioness of Stockbridge" or more simply, "The Marchioness of Stockbridge".

At the beginning of a letter, a marchioness would be addressed either as "Madam" or "Dear Lady (place-name)" for instance "Dear Lady Stockbridge".

On meeting a marchioness, she should be addressed "My lady" or "Your ladyship" or "Lady (place-name)".

Coronet and Mantle

A marquess's mantle has three-and-a-half rows of ermine on the cape. His coronet is a silver-gilt circlet with four silver strawberry leaves, as opposed to the duke's eight, the four intervening spaces being occupied by four silver balls – one in each space. The coronet has a cap of crimson velvet topped with a golden tassel, and is turned up with ermine.

The Children of Marquesses and Marchionsses

If a marquess has more than one title, his eldest son (known as the heir apparent) though not himself an actual peer, may use one of his father's lesser titles 'by courtesy'. For instance the Marquess of Anglesey also holds the title Earl of Uxbridge, and this title is generally given to the eldest son.

The wives of courtesy peers are also entitled to courtesy titles, which are the female equivalents of their husbands' titles, so the wife of the Earl of Uxbridge (a courtesy peer) would be styled Countess of Uxbridge. The children of the Earl and Countess of Uxbridge would also be entitled to use the same courtesy titles as the children of someone who is an Earl in his own right (see the section on Earls and Countesses for more information).

The actual courtesy title which is given to the eldest son of a marquess is a matter of family tradition, it does not necessarily have to be the highest title available.

If a marquess does not have any subsidiary titles of a name different from his main title, his eldest son usually uses the title "Lord (Surname)". This differs slightly from the title given to younger sons.

Another form of courtesy title is the honorific prefix of "(The) Lord" before the name, for instance The Lord John Smith. This non-peerage title is accorded to younger sons of marquesses. It does not, and has never, entitled a holder to sit in the House of Lords. The title may continue to be used after the death of the holder's father, but this courtesy title does not enable the children of Lords by courtesy to have titles of their own.

The wife of someone with a courtesy title is entitled to the feminine form of her husband's title, which takes the form of "(The) Lady", followed by her husband's name, for example Lady John Smith. The holder is addressed orally as "Lord John" or "My lord" and his wife is addressed orally as "Lady John" or "My Lady". In letters, the younger son of a marquess is addressed "My Lord" or "Dear Lord John", and his wife would be addressed "Madam" or "Dear Lady John".

The honorific prefix of "(The) Lady" is used for the daughters of marquesses. The courtesy title is added before the person's given name, so if Jane Smith is the daughter of a marquess, she may either be called The Lady Jane Smith, Lady Jane Smith, or Lady Jane (but not Lady Smith).

The title of Lady may still be used after the death of the holder's father but it is not inherited by her children. If Lady Jane Smith married Mr James

Fairfax, her husband would not gain any title by virtue of his marriage. Jane would however now be addressed as Lady Jane Fairfax.

Any woman who marries a peer uses the feminine version of his peerage title, even if her father's title is higher than her husband's, so should Lady Jane Smith marry Viscount Washington, she would become Viscountess Washington. This means that as a result of her marriage, she may drop down the order of precedence. (See Appendix D: Order of Precedence.)

In the case of a divorce, the former wife of a titled person may keep the title she acquired upon marriage, if she so wishes. So for instance, if Lord John Smith should marry more than once, there can be multiple Lady John Smiths.

If the mother is a marchioness in her own right (and the father holds a lower title or no title) the above rules still apply to their children.

Example

Let us say you were invited to the wedding of the Marquess of Stockbridge* and Miss Lavinia Vaughan-Williams, and you happily accepted the wedding invitation.

If you were asked to send your reply to the Marquess directly, you might address the envelope to "The Most Honourable the Marquess of Stockbridge", and could begin the letter of acceptance with "My Lord Marquess".

At the reception, after the wedding, if you were able to meet the Marquess and his wife, you might greet the Marquess as "Lord Stockbridge" and his wife as "Lady Stockbridge." Note that the marchioness should not be greeted as "Lady Lavinia" for the reason that "Lady (first name)" only applies to the daughters of dukes, marquesses and earls. It would, however, be acceptable to greet her as "My lady" or "Your ladyship."

*Note that as with the Duke and Duchess of Buckminster, the Marquess and Marchioness of Stockbridge are fictional titles.

If, years later, you were to meet their younger son, William, you might greet him as "Lord William." As with the daughter of a duke, mentioned in the last section, it may be the case that as a younger person, Lord William might feel more comfortable if his courtesy title was dropped, and may well prefer just to be called William. If you are able, you may discretely try and find this out in advance.

Earls and Countesses

Rank

An earl is the British equivalent of a continental count, and ranks above a viscount but below a marquess. Originally it was the highest rank, before the introduction of the titles duke and marquess in the fourteenth century.

The last earldom created was for Prince William who, as well as being made Duke of Cambridge, was also given the titles Earl of Strathearn and Baron Carrickfergus upon his marriage to Katherine Middleton in 2011. The last non-royal to be made an earl was former Prime Minister Harold Macmillan who, as well as being made Earl of Stockton in 1984, was also made Viscount Macmillan of Ovenden.

A woman who holds an earldom in her own right, or is the wife of an earl, is normally styled *countess*. An example of a countess in her own right, is Patricia Knatchbull, the 2nd Countess Mountbatten of Burma, inheriting the title from her father, Louis Mountbatten, 1st Earl Mountbatten of Burma. Her husband was also a peer (the 7th Baron Brabourne) and so together were one of the few couples to both hold peerages in their own right.

The husband of a countess in her own right, is *not* an

earl, unless he happens to already be a earl in his own right. If he was called Mr William Robinson before his marriage, he would continue to be called Mr William Robinson after his marriage.

If an earl divorces, his former wife is still entitled to be styled countess. Often she will use her first name before the title, for instance "Elizabeth, Countess of Newbury" to distinguish herself from any possible future countess, should the earl remarry.

If an earl dies, his surviving wife is still entitled to be called countess. However this may cause confusion if the heir to the peerage has a wife, who would also be styled countess. The widowed countess is therefore referred to either as the Dowager Countess or will use her first name before her title as above, for instance "Elizabeth, Countess of Newbury."

Forms of Address

On envelopes, an earl would usually be addressed as "(The Right Honourable) the Earl of (place-name)" for instance a letter might be addressed to "The Right Honourable the Earl of Carnarvon". However some earls are addressed "The Right Honourable the Earl (surname)" for instance the brother of Diana, Princess of Wales, would be formally addressed "The Right Honourable the Earl Spencer".

Earls by courtesy (i.e. those who are earls by virtue of their father being a peer) and the wives of earls by courtesy are not entitled to be referred to as "The Right Honourable" (unless the earl by courtesy also happens to be a privy counsellor – see Appendix C).

At the beginning of a letter, an earl would be addressed "My Lord" or "Dear Lord (place-name or surname)" depending on whether the peer is the Earl of (place-name) or Earl (surname).

On meeting an earl, he should be addressed "My lord" or "Your lordship" or "Lord (place-name or surname)".

Often a person on familiar terms with an earl would call him by the place-name in his title, rather than his actual name.

On envelopes, a countess would be addressed as "(The Right Honourable) the Countess of (place-name)" or "(The Right Honourable) the Countess (surname)".

At the beginning of a letter, a countess would be addressed to "Madam" or "Dear Lady (place-name or surname)".

On meeting a countess, she should be addressed "My lady" or "Your ladyship" or "Lady (place-name or surname)".

Coronet and Mantle

An earl's mantle has three rows of ermine on the cape. His coronet is a silver-gilt circlet with eight silver balls on points, and golden strawberry leaves between the points. The coronet has a cap of crimson velvet topped with a golden tassel, and is turned up with ermine.

The Children of Earls and Countesses

If an earl has more than one title, his eldest son (known as the heir apparent) though not himself an actual peer, may use one of his father's lesser titles 'by courtesy'.

The wives of courtesy peers are also entitled to courtesy titles, which are the female equivalents of their husbands' titles. The children of courtesy peers are also entitled to use courtesy titles, and would be styled *The Honourable.* This is because the heir apparent's title would be lower than that of his father, namely a viscountcy or barony, and the children of viscounts and barons are all styled *The Honourable.*

If an earl does not have any subsidiary titles (or he does but the place-name is the same as in his main title) his eldest son usually uses the title "Lord (Surname)". For instance the eldest son of the Earl of Devon is styled Lord Courtenay. This differs somewhat from the title given to younger sons.

Younger sons of earls are given the title "The Honourable". The title persists after the death of the holder's father, but this courtesy title does not enable the holder's children to have titles of their own.

The wife of someone with a courtesy title is entitled

to the feminine form of her husband's title, which, in the case of an earl's younger sons, takes the form of "The Honourable", followed by her title "Mrs" followed by her husband's name, so for example the wife of The Honourable John Smith would be "The Honourable Mrs John Smith".

Somewhat anomalously, the honorific prefix for the daughters of earls is not "The Honourable" as with the sons, but "(The) Lady". This courtesy title is added before the person's given name, so if Jane Smith is the daughter of an earl, she may either be called The Lady Jane Smith, Lady Jane Smith, or Lady Jane (but not Lady Smith).

The title of Lady may still be used after the death of the holder's father but it is not inherited by her children. If Lady Jane Smith married Mr James Fairfax, her husband would not gain any title by virtue of his marriage. Jane would however now be addressed as Lady Jane Fairfax.

Any woman who marries a peer uses the feminine version of his peerage title, even if her father's title is higher than her husband's, so should Lady Jane Smith marry Baron Vaynol, she would become Baroness Vaynol. This means that as a result of her marriage, she may drop down the order of precedence. (See Appendix D: Order of Precedence.)

In the case of a divorce, the former wife of a titled person may keep the title she acquired upon marriage, if she so wishes. So for instance, if the Honourable

John Smith should marry more than once, there can be multiple Honourable Mrs John Smiths.

If the mother is a countess in her own right, and the father is not of a higher rank, the above rules still apply to their children.

Cultural Example

In the popular television series *Downton Abbey,* Robert Crawley, Earl of Grantham, is the head of a fictional aristocratic family.

He is addressed by servants, and people such as the family physician, Dr Clarkson, as "Lord Grantham" or "My lord". Close friends and relatives refer to him generally as "Robert". It would not be a surprise if other lords, or old acquaintances referred to him simply as Grantham.

Robert's American wife, Cora, Countess of Grantham, is addressed as "Lady Grantham" or "My lady".

The earl and countess have three daughters: Lady Mary Crawley, Lady Edith Crawley and Lady Sybil Crawley (deceased). Lady Mary Crawley, for instance, is addressed as "Lady Mary" or "My lady". She is never addressed as "Lady Crawley" or "Lady Grantham".

Lady Sybil married the chauffeur, Tom Branson, who, as a man, is not entitled to any courtesy title by marriage and so remains Mr Tom Branson.

Lord Grantham has the subsidiary title "Viscount Downton", and when his father, the previous Earl, was alive, Robert was known as Viscount Downton.

Had Robert had any younger brothers, they would each have been given the courtesy title, The Honourable. Robert's sister is Lady Rosamund Painswick (née Crawley).

During the late nineteenth and the early twentieth centuries over a hundred wealthy American women came to Britain in search of a titled husband. Peers, impoverished by tax and falling crop prices, often married for the sake of their estates, rather than for love. The marriage of Robert and Cora, who was originally from Cincinnati, Ohio, reflects this trend, but their marriage, unlike so many of the time, is a happy one.

With this movement of wealthy American ladies from the United States to Britain during this period, a lot of today's English aristocracy have American ancestry. Winston Churchill (the grandson of a duke) and Diana, Princess of Wales (the daughter of an earl) were both partly of American descent.

Robert and Cora have no son, but they do have a grandson, George, who, though he is *likely* to become the next Earl of Grantham, is not entitled to Robert's subsidiary title. This is because George is not necessarily the heir – Robert could, theoretically, still have a son. This prospective son would then be the heir, and would likely be styled "Viscount Downton".

George is known as the heir presumptive, which means that he is currently in line to inherit both the title and estate, but there is a chance that he could lose this position should Robert have a legitimate son. If George had been Robert and Cora's eldest son, he would be known as the heir apparent, meaning that he is first in line to inherit the title and that he cannot be displaced from this position by the birth of another person.

Viscounts and Viscountesses

Rank

A viscount ranks above a baron but below an earl. The title comes from the French viscomte and means deputy count. (A count being the continental equivalent of an earl.)

As a rank of the British peerage, it was first recorded in 1440 when John Beaumont was created Viscount Beaumont by Henry VI.

Prince Edward, Earl of Wessex, was also made Viscount Severn in 1999 upon his marriage to Sophie Rhys-Jones. The last non-royal to be made a viscount was former Prime Minister Harold Macmillan who, as well as being made Earl of Stockton in 1984, was also made Viscount Macmillan of Ovenden.

A woman who holds a viscountcy in her own right, or is the wife of a viscount, is normally styled *viscountess*. A viscountess in her own right is very rare, and currently there are none.

The husband of a viscountess in her own right is *not* a viscount, unless he happens to already be a viscount in his own right. If he was called Mr Richard Brown before his marriage to a Viscountess, he would continue to be called Mr Richard Brown after his marriage.

If a viscount divorces, his former wife is still entitled to be styled viscountess. Often she will use her first name before the title, for instance "Christina, Viscountess of Newbury" to distinguish herself from any possible future viscountess, should the viscount remarry.

If a viscount dies, his surviving wife is still entitled to be called viscountess. However this may cause confusion if the heir to the peerage has a wife, who would also be styled viscountess. The widowed viscountess is therefore referred to either as the Dowager Viscountess or will use her first name before her title as above, for instance "Christina, Visountess of Newbury."

Forms of Address

On envelopes, a viscount would be addressed as "(The Right Honourable) the Viscount (place-name)" for instance a letter might be addressed to "The Right Honourable the Viscount Haversham" or "The Viscount Haversham". Note that it is almost never "Viscount *of* (place-name)" the two exceptions being the Viscount of Arbuthnott and the Viscount of Oxfuird. (Both of these are Scottish titles.)

Viscounts by courtesy (i.e. those who are viscounts by virtue of their father being a peer) and the wives of viscounts by courtesy are not entitled to be referred to as "The Right Honourable" (unless the viscount by courtesy also happens to be a privy counsellor – see Appendix C).

At the beginning of a letter, a viscount would be addressed "My Lord" or "Dear Lord (place-name)".

On meeting a viscount, he should be addressed "My lord" or "Your lordship" or "Lord (place-name)".

Often a person on familiar terms with a viscount would call him by the place-name in his title, rather than his actual name.

On envelopes, a viscountess would be addressed as

"(The Right Honourable) Viscountess (place-name)". Note, as above, that they are almost never addressed as the "Viscountess *of* (place-name)" the two exceptions being the Viscountess of Arbuthnott and the Viscountess of Oxfuird.

At the beginning of a letter, a viscountess would be addressed "Madam" or "Dear Lady (place-name)".

On meeting a viscountess, she should be addressed "My lady" or "Your ladyship" or "Lady (place-name)".

Coronet and Mantle

A viscount's mantle has two and a half bars of ermine on the cape. His coronet is a silver-gilt circlet with sixteen silver balls. As with other coronets, it has a cap of crimson velvet topped with a golden tassel, and is turned up with ermine.

The Children of Viscounts and Viscountesses

If a duke, marquess or earl has more than one title, his eldest son (known as the heir apparent) though not himself an actual peer, may use one of his father's lesser titles 'by courtesy'. This is not the case with viscounts – no subsidiary title, even if a viscount has one, may be used by the heir apparent.

Both the sons and daughters of viscounts use the courtesy titles "The Honourable (name)" – for instance The Honourable John Smith or The Honourable Jane Smith.

This courtesy title may still be used after the death of the holder's father, but having this courtesy title does not enable their children to have titles of their own.

The wife of someone with a courtesy title is entitled to the feminine form of her husband's title, which takes the form of "The Honourable", followed by her title "Mrs" followed by her husband's name, so for example the wife of The Honourable John Smith would be "The Honourable Mrs John Smith".

If a man with no honorific title, for instance Mr John Smith, marries a woman with the title "The

Honourable" he remains Mr John Smith.

In the case of a divorce, the wife of a viscount's son may keep the title she acquired upon marriage, if she so wishes. If The Honourable John Smith should marry more than once, there can be multiple The Honourable Mrs John Smiths.

If the mother is a viscountess in her own right, and the father is not of a higher rank, the above rules still apply to their children.

Cultural Example

The long running television series *Upstairs, Downstairs* followed the lives of the upper class Bellamy family ("Upstairs") and their servants ("Downstairs") during the Edwardian era.

Patriarch Richard Bellamy, married Lady Marjorie Talbot-Carey, who was entitled to the courtesy title "Lady", by virtue of being the daughter of the Earl of Southwold.

Though she has a courtesy title, this did not entitle her husband, Richard, or their children, Elizabeth and James, to any form of title.

The servants generally referred to Marjorie as "Lady Marjorie" when in conversation with one another, or "My Lady" when addressing her directly.

Five years after the death of Lady Marjorie (who perished with the Titanic in 1912) her husband, Richard, was elevated to the peerage, as a reward for his political contributions in the House of Commons, and was made Viscount Bellamy of Haversham.

After his ennoblement, the servants generally referred to Richard as "Lord Bellamy" when in conversation with one another, or "My Lord" when addressing him directly.

Lord Bellamy's second wife, Virginia, was generally referred to as "Lady Bellamy" or "My Lady".

Richard's daughter, Elizabeth, who had by this time left for America, would have the courtesy title of "The Honourable".

Richard's son, James, who was also an army Major, became, upon his father's ennoblement, Major The Honourable James Hugo Bellamy, MC. (MC being an abbreviation for the Military Cross, awarded to members of the armed forces for bravery.)

Servants generally referred to James as "The Major" when in conversation with one another, or "Sir" when addressing him directly. This is the same as prior to his father's ennoblement.

Barons and Baronesses

Rank

The rank of baron is the lowest, but oldest rank of the English (and British) peerage. The word baron comes from the Old French *Baron* which in turn comes from the Latin *baro* meaning soldier or servant. This word, in turn, may (though it is not certain) have come from the Frankish *beorn* meaning nobleman (or warrior). William I, that is, William the Conqueror, introduced the rank, bestowing it on men who had pledged their loyalty to him.

The last barony created was for Prince William who, as well as being made Duke of Cambridge, was also given the titles Earl of Strathearn and Baron Carrickfergus upon his marriage to Katherine Middleton in 2011. The last non-royal to be given a hereditary barony was John Morrison, who was made Baron Margadale in 1965.

A woman who holds the title to a barony in her own right, or is the wife of a baron, is normally styled *baroness*.

The husband of a baroness in her own right, is *not* a baron, unless he happens to already be a baron in his own right. If he was called Mr Edward Ford before his marriage, he would continue to be called Mr Edward

Ford after his marriage.

If a baron divorces, his former wife is still entitled to be styled baroness. Often she will use her first name before the title, for instance "Louisa, Baroness of Vaynol" to distinguish herself from any possible future baroness, should the baron remarry.

If a baron dies, his surviving wife is still entitled to be called baroness. However this may cause confusion if the heir to the peerage has a wife, who would also be styled baroness. The widowed baroness is therefore referred to either as the Dowager Baroness, or will use her first name before her title as above, for instance "Louisa, Baroness of Vaynol."

Please note that there is a separate section on life-peers who are all non-hereditary barons and baronesses. All the information in this section relates to hereditary baronies.

Forms of Address

On envelopes, a baron would be addressed as "(The Right Honourable) the Lord (place-name)". Note that hereditary barons are never addressed as Baron (place-name) except on certain legal documents. (It is a slightly different matter with baronesses.)

At the beginning of a letter, a baron would be addressed "My Lord" or "Dear Lord (place-name)".

On meeting a baron, he should be addressed "My lord" or "Your lordship" or "Lord (place-name)".

Often a person on familiar terms with a baron would call him by the place-name in his title, rather than his actual name.

Barons by courtesy (i.e. those who are barons by virtue of their father being a peer) and the wives of barons by courtesy are not entitled to be referred to as The Right Honourable (unless the baron by courtesy also happens to be a privy counsellor – See Appendix C).

On envelopes, a baroness in her own right would be addressed as "(The Right Honourable) Baroness (place-name)", or "(The Right Honourable) Lady (place-name)".

A baroness in her husband's right would be addressed "(The Right Honourable) Lady (place-name)". It would, however, be incorrect to address a baroness in her husband's right as "(The Right Honourable) Baroness (place-name)".

At the beginning of a letter, a Baroness (either in her own right or in her husband's right) would be addressed "Madam" or "Dear Lady (place-name)".

On meeting a baroness, she should be addressed "Your ladyship" or "Lady (place-name)".

Coronet and Mantle

A baron's mantle has two bars of ermine on the cape. His coronet is a silver-gilt circlet with six large silver balls, called pearls. As with other peers' coronets, a baron's coronet has a cap of crimson velvet topped with a golden tassel, and is turned up with ermine.

On a coat of arms, four of the six pearls would be visible on the coronet.

The Children of Barons and Baronesses

If a duke, marquess or earl has more than one title, his eldest son (known as the heir apparent) though not himself an actual peer, may use one of his father's lesser titles 'by courtesy'. This is not the case with barons (or viscounts) – no subsidiary title, even if a baron has one, may be used by the heir apparent. It is very rare for barons to have two titles. One example, though, is the Scottish peer, Baron Stratheden, who is also Baron Campbell.

Both the sons and daughters of barons use the courtesy titles "The Honourable (name)" – for instance The Honourable John Smith or The Honourable Jane Smith.

This courtesy title may still be used after the death of the holder's father, but having this courtesy title does not enable their children to have titles of their own.

The wife of someone with a courtesy title is entitled to the feminine form of her husband's title, which takes the form of "The Honourable", followed by her title "Mrs" followed by her husband's name, so for example the wife of The Honourable John Smith would be "The

Honourable Mrs John Smith".

If a man with no honorific title, for instance Mr John Jackson, marries a woman with the title "The Honourable" he remains Mr John Jackson.

In the case of a divorce, the wife of a baron's son may keep the title she acquired upon marriage, if she so wishes. If The Honourable John Smith should marry more than once, there can be multiple The Honourable Mrs John Smiths.

If the mother is a baroness in her own right, and the father is not of a higher rank, the above rules still apply to their children.

Example

Imagine you are invited to tea with the Honourable Elizabeth Carstairs, the unmarried daughter of Lord and Lady Vaynol*.

If you decided to accept the invitation, you would address your letter of reply to The Honourable Elizabeth Carstairs. If you knew her well, you might omit the courtesy title.

You would begin the letter with "Dear Miss Carstairs".

Upon meeting your host, you might address her formally as Miss Carstairs, or informally as Elizabeth, depending on how well you knew her. You would not call her "The Honourable Miss Carstairs."

You would address her father as Lord Vaynol and her mother as Lady Vaynol. You would not address them as Baron and Baroness Vaynol.

As with other examples, Lord and Lady Vaynol are fictional titles.

Life Peers

Rank

Life peers are the holders of non-hereditary peerages. Such titles were rare before the twentieth century. Perhaps not surprisingly, after the effective cessation of creating new hereditary peers, the number of life peers grew rapidly. The main point of change came about with the Life Peerages Act of 1958, which sanctioned the creating of unlimited life peers. Within seven years of the Act, as well as a steep rise in *life* peerages being granted, the awarding of *hereditary* peerages had effectively ceased.

Life peerages are given by the monarch on advice from the Prime Minister. They are normally given to politicians who formerly sat in the House of Commons, but they are sometimes awarded to other people who have had distinguished careers, such as businessmen and women, scientists and so on.

A number of hereditary peerages were created in the 1950s and 1960s so that the recipients of these honours could sit in the House of Lords. In 1999, hereditary peers could no longer sit in the House of Lords as of right, so many of these hereditary peers were also given life peerages so they could continue to attend the House of Lords. For instance, Toby Low was made

1st Baron Aldington in 1962 (a hereditary peerage) and granted a life peerage as Baron Low in 1999 so that he could remain in the House of Lords.

While the Peerage Act of 1963 allows hereditary peers to disclaim their title (see Appendix A for more information) there is no such provision for life peers.

The most important part of the Life Peerages act of 1958 was that it allowed women to sit in the Lords for the first time. Before this, even female hereditary peers in their own right could not participate in debates in the Lords. Today, around 20% of life peers are female.

Forms of Address

All new life peers to date have been given the rank of baron. As with hereditary peers, they are formally addressed in The House of Lords as "The Noble Lord" or, for women, "The Noble Baroness" or "The Noble Lady".

Male life peers are addressed Lord (surname) or, more rarely, Lord (place-name), an example of each being Lord Coe, and Lord Deben. Female life peers are titled Lady (surname) or Baroness (surname) or either, for instance, after being ennobled, Margaret Thatcher was usually referred to as Baroness Thatcher, but was also regularly addressed as Lady Thatcher.

If two barons or baronesses share a surname they sometimes distinguish themselves from one another by using a place-name, for instance Baroness Kennedy of The Shaws.

On envelopes, a baron would be addressed as "(The Right Honourable) the Lord (surname *or* place-name)".

At the beginning of a letter, a baron would be addressed "My Lord" or "Dear Lord (surname *or* place-name)".

On meeting a baron they should be addressed "My

lord" or "Your lordship" or "Lord (surname *or* place-name)".

On envelopes, a baroness in her own right would be addressed as "(The Right Honourable) Baroness (surname *or* place-name)", or "(The Right Honourable) Lady (surname *or* place-name)".

A baroness in her husband's right would be addressed "(The Right Honourable) Lady (surname *or* place-name)". It would be incorrect to address a baroness in her husband's right as "(The Right Honourable) Baroness (surname *or* place-name)".

At the beginning of a letter, a Baroness (either in her own right, or in her husband's right) would be addressed "Madam" or "Dear Lady (surname *or* place-name)".

On meeting a baroness (in her own right, or in her husband's right) she should be addressed "Your ladyship" or "Lady (surname *or* place-name)".

Coronet and Mantle

A life peer is entitled to wear the same coronet and mantle as a hereditary baron. As mentioned in the previous chapter, a baron's mantle has two bars of ermine on the cape. His coronet is a silver-gilt circlet with six large silver balls. As with other peers' coronets, a baron's coronet has a cap of crimson velvet topped with a golden tassel, and is turned up with ermine.

With life peers, unlike hereditary peers, there are a large numbers of peeresses (female peers). They are also entitled to wear coronets, though theirs are generally smaller than those worn by their male counterparts. Peeresses' coronation robes also include trains, which signify rank by length and the width of ermine around the train.

Ede and Ravenscroft, who make robes for peers, have more information on peers' ceremonial clothing: www.edeandravenscroft.com

The Children of Life Peers

If a life peer has another, lower or equivalent title, this title cannot be passed down. This passing down of subsidiary titles only applies to dukes, marquesses and earls.

Both the sons and daughters of barons use the courtesy titles "The Honourable (name)" – for instance The Honourable John Smith or The Honourable Jane Smith.

This courtesy title may still be used after the death of the holder's father, but having this courtesy title does not enable the courtesy title holder's children to have titles of their own.

The wife of someone with a courtesy title is entitled to the feminine form of her husband's title, which takes the form of "The Honourable", followed by her title "Mrs" followed by her husband's name, so for example the wife of The Honourable John Smith would be "The Honourable Mrs John Smith".

If a man with no honorific title, for instance Mr John Jones, marries a woman with the title "The Honourable" he remains Mr John Jones.

In case of a divorce, the wife of a life peer's son may keep the title she acquired upon marriage, if she so wishes. If The Honourable John Smith should marry more than once, there can be multiple The Honourable Mrs John Smiths.

If the mother is a life peer in her own right, and the father is not of a higher rank, the above rules still apply to their children. For instance Baroness Thatcher's son, Mark Thatcher, is entitled to the courtesy title "The Honourable".

Part 2: Titled People Below the Ranks of the Peerage

Baronets and Baronetesses

Rank

Baronets rank below the five ranks of the peerage. They are not peers and so have never been able to sit in the House of Lords (unless they also held, or later acquired, a peerage). Baronets have been able to sit in the House of Commons, if elected, and one recent example is Sir George Young, Bt, who was first elected to the House of Commons in 1974. Baronets are sometimes referred to as the sixth division of the aristocracy. (See, for instance:

www.baronetage.org/a-short-history).

Baronets rank above knights – with two exceptions, namely: Knights of the Garter and Knights of the Thistle. (Baronets were also ranked below The Most Illustrious Order of Saint Patrick, but this Irish order of chivalry is now obsolete.)

A baronet is the holder of a hereditary baronetcy awarded by the monarch. Baronets have existed since at least the 1300s, and at the beginning of the 17th century, James I of England conferred a large number of baronetcies. There was a condition attached, however – those receiving the honour had to pay for the upkeep of up to thirty soldiers, for three years, at a cost of over £1000 – well over £100,000 today.

A large number of baronetcies were also created in the nineteenth century, when it was thought that the House of Lords was too full to admit new members.

Though baronets are styled *Sir,* they are not, as is sometimes believed, hereditary knights.

Since 1965, only one new baronetcy has been created, for Margaret Thatcher's husband, Dennis, in 1991.

There have only been four baronetesses in their own right. (Note that the wife of a baronet is not a baronetess.) No baronetesses exist as of 2014, and the last baronetess, Dame Anne Macdonald, died in 2011.

Today there are around 1200 baronetcies still in existence.

Forms of Address

On envelopes, a baronet would be addressed as "Sir (name), bt" or "Sir (name), bart". Bt and Bart being abbreviations of baronet. Bt is the modern convention, and Bart is a more old-fashioned term. Bt or Bart is written after the name to show that the person in question is a baronet rather than a knight. So for instance one might address a letter to Sir John Smith, Bt.

At the beginning of a letter, a baronet named John Smith would be addressed "Sir" or "Dear Sir John" or "Dear Sir John Smith".

On meeting a baronet, he should be addressed "Sir" or "Sir John", but never as "Sir Smith".

On envelopes, a baronet's wife would be addressed as "Lady (surname)".

At the beginning of a letter, a baronet's wife would be addressed "Madam" or "Dear Lady (surname)".

On meeting a baronet's wife they should be addressed "My lady" or "Lady (surname)".

On envelopes, a baronetess in her own right would be addressed as "Dame (name), Btss" for example "Dame

Isobel Smith, Btss". (Btts being the abbreviation for Baronetess.)

At the beginning of a letter, a baronetess would be addressed "Madam" or "Dear Dame (name)" for instance "Dear Dame Isobel Smith" or "Dear Dame Isobel".

On meeting a baronetess, she should be addressed "Madam" or "Dame (first-name)".

The husband of a baronetess does not acquire any title upon marrying a baronetess. If he was Mr Brian Deacon before the marriage, he will remain Mr Brian Deacon after the marriage.

If the wife of a baronet divorces her husband, she is entitled to keep her title, but should put her first name before her title, for instance "Jane, Lady Smith", to distinguish herself from any possible future Lady Smith, should the baronet remarry.

If a baronet dies, his surviving wife is still entitled to be called "Lady (surname)", unless the heir remarries. In this case she would normally be called "Dowager Lady (surname)" or "(first-name), Lady (surname)", for example "Jane, Lady Smith", to distinguish herself from her daughter-in-law.

There are rare occasions when someone may be entitled to two different titles. A current example is Mark Thatcher, who was entitled to use the title "The Honourable" after his mother, former Prime Minister,

Margaret Thatcher, was made a life peer.

As his father, Dennis, was also created a baronet, then, upon his father's death, Mark was also able to use the prefix "Sir" and so is now titled The Honourable Sir Mark Thatcher, 2nd Baronet.

As mentioned above, since 1965, only one new baronetcy has been created, for Margaret Thatcher's husband, Dennis, in 1991. This was the last hereditary title to be given to a British subject.

Coronet and Mantle

Baronets are not entitled to wear a coronet and mantle, and should not have a coronet on their coat of arms. However, there *may* be rare exceptions to this, for instance in *Burke's Peerage and Baronetage (107th Edition)* the arms of the Agnew-Somerville baronets show the family shield surmounted by a baron's coronet.

The Children of Baronets and Baronetesses

The children of baronets and baronetesses are not given any courtesy titles on the basis of their parent being either a baronet or baronetess. However the title of baronet, or baronetess may be passed down, usually to the eldest son, or, rarely, to more distant male relatives or, more rarely still, it may be inherited by a female relative.

Knights and Dames

Rank

Generally ranking lower than peers and baronets, knights were, during the middle ages, considered as making up a lower class of the aristocracy, and Thomas Malory's Le *Morte d'Arthur* did a lot to popularize the concept of the knight as a warrior, closely allied to the king or to a lord. Often medieval knights served lords and were paid with land.

The word knight derives from the German word *Knecht* meaning servant or bondsman. In Old English it meant adolescent or servant. In the 1100s, the meaning of knight began to change from a young male servant to warrior. By 1300 the idea of knights fighting on horseback, emerged during the Hundred Years' War (1337 – 1453).

From the mid-sixteenth century knighthoods were awarded less to soldiers for gallantry, and more as a reward to civilians for services rendered to society. This is still the case as of the early twenty-first century.

In more recent times, the title of dame has been conferred on women who have made a significant contribution to British society. The title of dame ranks equivalently with the title of knight.

There are different kinds of knighthoods (and

damehoods) and are ranked in descending order as follows:

The Most Noble Order of the Garter:

Created in 1348, the Order of the Garter is the oldest and most prestigious of all the orders of chivalry. A man who is awarded this honour is called a Knight of the Garter, and, as well as the title "Sir", is also able to use the post nominal letters KG. A woman who is awarded this honour is called a Lady of the Garter, and, as well as the title "Lady", is also able to use the post nominal letters LG. This rank is limited to twenty five people at any one time.

The motto is: *Honi soit qui mal y pense* (Shame on him who thinks this evil)

The Most Ancient and Noble Order of the Thistle:

Created during the reign of James II, the Order of the Thistle has ancient roots, but was only formally established by James II in 1687. A man who is awarded this honour is called a Knight of the Thistle, and, as well as the title "Sir", is also able to use the post nominal letters KT. A woman who is awarded this honour is called a Lady of the Thistle, and, as well as the title "Lady", is also able to use the post nominal letters LT. This rank is limited to sixteen people, all of whom must be Scottish.

The motto is: *Nemo me impune lacessit* (No one provokes me with impunity)

The Order of Merit:

Though not a knighthood, the Order of Merit ranks alongside knighthoods and so is included here. This order was created in 1902 to recognise those who had contributed to science, art, music, literature or public life. A person awarded this honour is known as a Member of the Order of Merit, and is entitled to use the post nominal letters OM. The rank is limited to twenty four people.

The Royal Victorian Order:

Created in 1896, the Royal Victorian Order, or RVO for short, is given for services to the monarch and other members of the Royal Family. There are five levels of award, namely:

1 – Knight/Dame Grand Cross
2 – Knight/Dame Commander

3 – Commander
4 – Lieutenant
5 – Member

Only the first two of these are knighthoods. A man who is made a Knight Grand Cross, as well as being styled "Sir", is also able to use the post nominal letters GCVO. A woman who is made a Dame Grand Cross, as well as being styled "Dame", is also able to use the same post nominal letters GCVO.

A man who is made a Knight Commander, as well as being styled "Sir", is also able to use the post nominal letters KCVO. A woman who is made a Dame Commander, as well as being styled "Dame", is able to use the post nominal letters DCVO.

Though the following honours are not knighthoods, a little information has been included here, in case the reader is interested:

A Commander is entitled to the post nominal letters CVO.

A Lieutenant is entitled to the post nominal letters LVO.

A Member is entitled to the post nominal letters MVO.

The Most Honourable Order of the Bath:

Created in 1725, the Most Honourable Order of the

Bath, like the Order of the Thistle, has ancient roots. Its name came about in the middle ages, and is derived from the ceremonial bathing that preceded the investiture. There are three levels of award, namely:

1 – Knight/Dame Grand Cross
2 – Knight/Dame Commander
3 – Companion

Only the first two of these are knighthoods. A man who is made a Knight Grand Cross, as well as being styled "Sir", is also able to use the post nominal letters GCB. A woman who is made a Dame Grand Cross, as well as being styled "Dame", is also able to use the same post nominal letters GCB.

A man who is made a Knight Commander, as well as being styled "Sir", is also able to use the post nominal letters KCB. A woman who is made a Dame Commander, as well as being styled "Dame", is also able to use the post nominal letters DCB.

The honour of being made a Companion, though not a knighthood, entitles the recipient to use the post nominal letters CB.

The motto is: *Tria Juncta in Uno* (Three joined in one)

The Order of St Michael and St George:

Created in 1818, this order was created to reward service in Malta and the Ionian islands. Today it may be awarded to anyone in the Diplomatic Service for an outstanding contribution. There are three levels of award, namely:

1 – Knight/Dame Grand Cross
2 – Knight/Dame Commander
3 – Companion

Only the first two of these are knighthoods. A man who is made a Knight Grand Cross, as well as being styled "Sir", is also able to use the post nominal letters GCMG. A woman who is made a Dame Grand Cross, as well as being styled "Dame", is also able to use the same post nominal letters GCMG.

A man who is made a Knight Commander, as well as being styled "Sir", is also able to use the post nominal letters KCMG. A woman who is made a Dame Commander, as well as being styled "Dame", is also able to use the post nominal letters DCMG.

The honour of being made a Companion entitles the recipient to use the post nominal letters CMG.

The motto is: *Auspicium Melioris Aevi* (Token of a better age)

The Order of the British Empire:

Instituted by George V in 1917, these awards are perhaps the most well-known honours today, regularly being conferred on well-known people who have made outstanding contributions to their field, such as sport or entertainment. There are five levels of award, namely:

1 – Knight/Dame Grand Cross of the Most Excellent Order of the British Empire
2 – Knight/Dame Commander of the Most Excellent Order of the British Empire
3 – Commander of the Most Excellent Order of the British Empire
4 – Officer of the Most Excellent Order of the British Empire
5 – Member of the Most Excellent Order of the British Empire

Only the first two of these are knighthoods. A man who is made a Knight Grand Cross, as well as being styled "Sir", is also able to use the post nominal letters GBE. A woman who is made a Dame Grand Cross, as well as being styled "Dame", is also able to use the same post nominal letters GBE.

A man who is made a Knight Commander, as well as being styled "Sir", is also able to use the post nominal letters KBE. A woman who is made a Dame Commander, as well as being styled "Dame", is also able to use the post nominal letters DBE.

Though the following honours are not knighthoods, they have been included in case the reader is interested:

A Commander of the Most Excellent Order of the British Empire is entitled to the post nominal letters CBE.

An Officer of the Most Excellent Order of the British Empire is entitled to the post nominal letters OBE.

A Member of the Most Excellent Order of the British Empire is entitled to the post nominal letters MBE.

There is also the British Empire Medal (BEM) which ranks below and MBE. Someone who is awarded a British Empire Medal is entitled to use the post nominal letters BEM.

Information on how to nominate someone for an honour is included in Appendix A.

Knight Bachelor:

There are other awards besides those listed above, but most of these are beyond the scope of this book. The only other award that needs mentioning is the Knight Bachelor. Originating in medieval times, this entitles the recipient to the prefix "Sir", but they are not entitled to use post nominal letters. This award is only conferred on men. Women are instead awarded the DBE. This is somewhat anomalous as the DBE (or its equivalent the KBE) is of a higher rank than that of Knights Bachelor.

Knights Bachelor rank below all the knights of the various orders listed above, but above the ranks of CBE, OBE, MBE and BEM.

A Note on the Rank of Baronets

As mentioned previously, baronets rank above all knights except The Most Noble Order of the Garter and The Most Ancient and Noble Order of the Thistle (and the obsolete The Most Illustrious Order of Saint Patrick).

Forms of Address

On envelopes, a knight would be addressed as "Sir (name)".

At the beginning of a letter, a knight would be addressed "Sir" or "Dear Sir (first name)".

On meeting a knight, he should be addressed "Sir" or "Sir (name)".

A knight such as Paul McCartney, could be addressed orally or at the beginning of a letter as Sir, or Sir Paul, or Sir Paul McCartney, but never Sir McCartney. As well as being made a Knight Bachelor in 1997, Sir Paul was awarded an MBE in 1965, so he may be addressed orally, or on envelopes, as Sir Paul McCartney, MBE.

On envelopes, a knight's wife would be addressed as "Lady (surname)".

At the beginning of a letter, a knight's wife would be addressed "Madam" or "Dear Lady (surname)".

On meeting a knight's wife she should be addressed "My lady" or "Lady (surname)".

On envelopes, a dame would be addressed as "Dame (name)" for instance Dame Jane Smith.

At the beginning of a letter, a dame would be addressed "Madam" or "Dear Dame (first name)" or "Dear Dame (name)" for instance "Dear Dame Jane" or "Dear Dame Jane Smith".

On meeting a dame they should be addressed "Madam" or "Dame (first name)".

The husband of a dame does not acquire any title upon marrying her. If he was Mr James Thompson before the marriage, he will remain Mr James Thompson after the marriage.

There is one exception to the rule on addressing knights and dames and that is for a woman who has been awarded *The Most Noble Order of the Garter* or *The Most Ancient and Noble Order of the Thistle*. In this case she is entitled to the title *Lady*.

On envelopes, a woman who has been awarded *The Most Noble Order of the Garter* or *The Most Ancient and Noble Order of the Thistle* would be addressed as "Lady (name)" for instance Lady Jane Smith.

At the beginning of a letter, she would be addressed "Madam" or "Dear Lady (name)" or "Dear Lady (first name)" for instance "Dear Lady Jane Smith" or "Dear Lady Jane".

On meeting a female recipient of *The Most Noble Order of the Garter* or *The Most Ancient and Noble Order of the Thistle*, she should be addressed "My Lady" or "Lady (first name)".

This has some resemblance to the daughters of dukes, marquesses and earls, who also have the courtesy tilte of "Lady" before their first name. All other women who have the prefix "Lady" have this as a result of marriage, and would either be known as Lady (surname), for instance Lady Smith, or Lady (husband's name), for instance Lady James Armitage.

Coronet and Mantle

As with baronets, knights and dames are not entitled to wear a coronet and mantle, and should not have a coronet on their coat of arms. In Continental Europe, there have been hereditary knighthoods (unlike in the United Kingdom), and these hereditary knights have sometimes been entitled to display a coronet on their coat of arms.

The Children of Knights and Dames

The children of knights and dames are not entitled to any courtesy title. Knighthoods, unlike baronetcies and hereditary peerages, cannot be inherited. In Continental Europe, knighthoods have occasionally been passed down, but this is more akin to baronetcies in the United Kingdom.

Miscellaneous
Ranks and Titles

Lords of the Manor

Though not an aristocratic title as such, there are similarities between lords of the manor and titled aristocrats, with land, titles and a long history often being an integral part of lordships of the manor.

The origins of lordships of manors, date back to Anglo-Saxon times, when the lord of the manor would receive a rental income from the tenants that lived and worked on his land. He would also act as judge in disputes between tenants.

The owner of a lordship of the manor may be described as (name), Lord/Lady of the Manor of (place-name), for instance Jane Smith, Lady of the Manor of Beaumaris, or in shortened form Jane Smith, Lady of Beaumaris. The children of a lord or lady of the manor are not entitled to any form of title.

Historically, from the seventeenth to the twentieth centuries, many lords of the manor were of upper class stock. Often their house, land and title had been passed down the family for centuries. Lords of the manor were generally part of the gentry, and were not referred to as "Lord" but instead referred to as "Squire". (The term "squire" was also applied to other landed upper class gentlemen who were the heads of large estates, not just lords of the manor.)

As with peers, and other people who owned large amounts of land at the beginning of the twentieth century, death duties have significantly eroded the land-ownership and power of lords of the manor, and today lords of the manor generally have little influence over local issues. That is not to say they have absolutely no influence, and newspaper articles have cropped up from time-to-time in recent years highlighting cases where purchasers of such titles have tried to extract money from tenants, citing ancient rights.

Unlike peerages and baronetcies, lordships of manors may be bought. These entitle the purchaser to the title, as mentioned above, and usually involve the purchase of large amounts of land as well as a manor house. As the title is not bestowed but bought, a person of any nationality may purchase a lordship of the manor. A British national may, if they wish, have the title Lord (or Lady) of the manor put on their passport. Many other citizens may or may not have the title put on their passport, for instance, in Canada it is allowed, whereas in the United States and in Australia, it is not.

The title, unlike most peerages and baronetcies, may pass down both male and female lines. Despite the prefix "Lord" it is not a noble title. Indeed there has been much debate on the validity of this title. If a man rented out a room in his house, or owned a pub, he would be a "landlord", but this title has no special merit or value. John Martin Robinson, co-author of *The Oxford Guide to Heraldry* famously remarked that the "Lordship of this or that manor is no more a title than Landlord of The Dog and Duck."

Though this remark is legally correct, lordships of manors have a long history, and were generally made up of landed gentry who were just outside, or on the fringes of, the English aristocracy.

A cultural example of a Lady of the Manor, is the upper-class Audrey fforbes-Hamilton [sic], in the BBC comedy series, *To the Manor Born*, which ran from 1979 to 1981.

A real life example of a Lord of the Manor, who is also an aristocrat, is Hugh Lowther, 8th Earl of Lonsdale, Viscount Lowther, Baron of Whitehaven and Lord of the Manor of Threlkeld.

(Stop Press: At the time of publication, the Earl of Lonsdale is selling Blencathra, a mountain which has formed part of the Lowther family's estate for 400 years. The mountain is being sold for around £1.75 million, or $3 million. The title of Lord of the Manor of Threlkeld comes with the land. According to the advertisement, the new holder of this title may also apply to the College of Arms for a coat of arms.)

Landed Gentry

The landed gentry were made up of upper class families who owned enough land to live off the rental income derived from tenants, and from the food produced on their lands. They often held smaller amounts of land than peers, and lived in less grand houses, though they could on occasions be wealthier than peers.

The most significant difference between the gentry and the aristocracy, was that the landed gentry lacked titles. The landed gentry were, however, armigerous, that is they had coats of arms.

Some books classify baronets and knights as making up the upper echelons of the landed gentry. Elsewhere the untitled landed gentry are referred to as "minor aristocracy". This is because, whereas peerages, baronetcies and so on are fairly well-defined, terms such as "aristocracy" and "gentry" have no legal definition, and have fluid meanings. As mentioned in the introduction, this book assumes aristocracy to cover peers, baronets, knights and their families, but because the landed gentry could be seen as making up the lower rungs of the aristocracy, this short chapter on the landed gentry has been included.

For centuries, when only the rich could enter politics, members of the landed gentry made up a large proportion of the House of Commons, while peers sat in the House of Lords. Today, a man or woman from any social background may stand to be elected to the House of Commons, and may be elevated to the House of Lords as a life peer.

At the beginning of the twenty first century, many houses of the landed gentry are still scattered across the country, but in most cases much of the land has been sold off, to pay death duties (inheritance tax), and when these houses are sold they now tend to come with just a few acres of land, rather than hundreds or even thousands of acres, as would have been the case a century or two ago.

Gentry, who were neither baronets, nor knights, could be given the ranks of esquire or gentleman, both of which are recognised in law. Esquire ranks above a gentleman but below a knight, though today any man of good habits, regardless of background may be considered a gentleman, and any man without a title is entitled to have "esquire" written after his name as a courtesy, on envelopes.

Part 3: Appendices

Appendix A: Frequently Asked Questions

If the titled person also has another title (academic, military and so on) which title comes first?

Generally the academic, clerical, military, etc, title comes first, for example General Sir Henry Jones, or Dr Sir John Smith. If someone is a Lord and they also have another title, they are normally referred to solely by their noble title. They can be referred to both titles, if they so wish, so someone who holds two titles may wish to be called Professor Lord Smith, but more often than not the title of Professor would be dropped.

In the television series *Upstairs, Downstairs,* Richard Bellamy is made a viscount. His son, James Bellamy, who is an army Major, becomes, upon his father's ennoblement, Major The Honourable James Hugo Bellamy, MC.

Can titles be bought?

Sometimes misleading adverts are put out, stating that titles can be bought, and the fees charged are often hefty. Usually this process simply involves changing one's name, e.g. from John Smith to Lord John Smith, but this is merely a change of name, not title, and the person would be known legally as Mr Lord John Smith.

Under Prime Minister Lloyd George, at the beginning of the twentieth century, many titles were sold. This was at a time the selling of titles was not illegal.

Viscountcies were sold for around £100,000 (around £4 million today) and knighthoods were sold for £10,000 - £15,000 (around half a million pounds today). Baronetcies cost around £30,000 (over a million pounds today). This eventually led to the Honours (Prevention of Abuses) Act 1925, which made the sale of honours illegal.

Still, rumours persist of honours, while not being sold, being instead given in return for donations to political parties.

The title of Lord (or Lady) of the Manor can be bought legally, but it has no real status and forms no part of the ranks of titles and honours. There is a section, not too many pages back, giving some more information on Lordships of the Manor.

Can titles be conferred retrospectively?

This has happened on occasions. For instance Edward Courtenay, 1st Earl of Devon (1527-1556) died unmarried and childless, and it was thought the title had become extinct. However, in 1831, a distant relative, William Courtenay, the 2nd Viscount Courtenay, successfully petitioned for the title of Earl of Devon to be restored. He was given the restored title and made 9th Earl of Devon, and his deceased forebears were retrospectively made Earls.

The Committee for Privileges, who look into such matters, has, since 1927, had the power to deny such a claim if the peerage has been in abeyance for more than one hundred years.

If someone outside the British Commonwealth is made a knight, is he allowed to be addressed with the prefix "Sir"?

No, is the short answer. Bill Gates was made a Knight Commander, but cannot be addressed as Sir Bill Gates, unless he becomes a citizen of the British Commonwealth. He can, however, use the post-nominal letters KBE, and may be addressed in writing as Bill Gates, KBE. Similarly the wife of Bill Gates could not be called Lady Gates.

Radio and television presenter, Terry Wogan, an Irish citizen, was awarded an honorary KBE in 2005. He later became a British citizen, and was subsequently allowed to be styled Sir Terry Wogan.

Can people renounce their titles?

Yes, this can be done. For instance peers, until recently, could not sit in the House of Commons which, since the early twentieth century, had been, and continues to be, far more powerful than the House of Lords.

Peers wishing to stand for election to the House of Commons, have renounced their titles. The most famous peer to do this was Tony Benn, who was elected to the House of Commons in 1950. On the death of his father, the first Viscount Stansgate, in 1960, Tony Benn became the second Viscount Stangate and was thus barred from the House of Commons. After protesting for three years, The Peerage Act became law at 6pm on 31st of July 1963. At 6.22pm that same day, Tony Benn renounced his title, and was later elected to the House of Commons.

Tony Benn was able to renounce his title, but after his death in March 2014, just over half a century after renouncing his title, Tony Benn's eldest son, Stephen Michael Wedgewood Benn, inherited the Viscountcy and became the third Viscount Stansgate.

Can people be stripped of their titles?

Yes. A recent example being the former Chief Executive Officer of the Royal Bank of Scotland, Fred Goodwin, whose knighthood was annulled in February 2012. (The Royal Bank of Scotland made a loss of over £24 billion in 2008 under his stewardship.)

There is more information on the removal of honours on the following government web-page:

www.gov.uk/honours/having-honours-taken-away

If a peer renounced his title, would his children still be allowed to use their courtesy titles?

Yes, is the straight forward answer. It may even be possible for children to later inherit their father's title even though it has been renounced. (See the question "Can people renounce their titles?" a couple of pages back.) The children of someone who has renounced his title do have the option of also dropping their courtesy titles.

Unlike any children she may have, the wife of a peer who renounced his title, would also lose her title.

Can I nominate someone for an honour?

Yes, people can nominate others for honours. Contact details can be found in Appendix B, under *Honours and Appointments*. Please note that you do not choose the honour that you wish to nominate someone for – this is decided by the honours committee.

The honours that may be awarded include Companion of Honour, GBE, KBE/DBE, CBE, OBE, MBE, BEM and RVO. Nominated people will not be awarded hereditary peerages or baronetcies as these are no longer given.

There is a slightly different system for nominations for life peerages, where people may, if they wish, nominate themselves. There is more information on this in Appendix B, under *Appointments to the House of Lords*.

Isn't it unfair, especially in these days of apparent gender equality, that a woman may gain a title by virtue of her husband having one, but not the other way round?

In the past, very few women were awarded any sort of title, and even today women make up only twenty percent of the members of the House of Lords. Historically, with only men, by and large, receiving honours, it perhaps did not seem particularly wrong to let their wives also gain a title. Today, however, more women than ever are receiving titles, and it does now seem anomalous that a woman may still acquire a title by virtue of her husband having one, but not the other way round.

There has been much talk of men being entitled to some sort of title, if their wife has one. One suggestion has been to give the husband of a titled woman the title of The Honourable. There has also been the suggestion that the wives (of knights at least) should not gain any title, and should remain Mrs.

An excellent article on the current honours system, by Chris Gash, including the tricky question on spouses receiving titles from their partners, may be found online:

www.publications.parliament.uk/pa/cm200304/cmsele
ct/cmpubadm/212/212we48.htm

Information on this gender inequality can be found on
the above link, in section 2.6.

If an heir apparent is given up for adoption, is he entitled to inherit the title upon the death of his biological father?

Yes. I'm not sure if this has ever happened, but the heir apparent would still be entitled to inherit the title.

Similarly, and conversely, if a boy was adopted by a peer the boy may gain the courtesy title of "Lord" or "The Honourable" by virtue of the adoption and their adopted father's title, but he would not be able to inherit the peerage even if he was older than any biological son, or even the only son, of the peer.

Appendix B: Contact Information

College of Arms

If you wish to apply for a coat of arms you would need to apply via *The College of Arms*. Their address is:

The College of Arms
130 Queen Victoria Street
London
EC4V 4BT

Before applying, it is probably best to visit their website and read up on their criteria, the address being:

www.college-of-arms.gov.uk

The Hereditary Peerage Association

The Hereditary Peerage Association was formed in 2002 three years after the House of Lords Act 1999, under which all by ninety-two hereditary peers were deprived of their seats in the House of Lords. Information can be found on their website:

www.hereditarypeers.com

Note that most of the information here is written by peers for peers, rather than for the general public, but it does contain a lot of useful information on the latest laws relating to peers and the House of Lords.

Honours and Appointments

If you wish to nominate someone for an honour, you are best off reading the information on:

www.gov.uk/honours

You can also telephone the Honours and Appointments Secretariat on 020 7276 2777 or, if you prefer, you can write to:

Honours and Appointments Secretariat
Cabinet Office
Ground Floor
Room G39
1 Horse Guards Road
London
SW1A 2HQ

Appointments to the House of Lords

People can be nominated to become life peers, and may even nominate themselves. Anyone who is interested in becoming a life peer, or nominating someone, should visit:

lordsappointments.independent.gov.uk

You can also write to:

House of Lords Appointment Commission
G/7, Ground Floor
1 Horse Guards Road
London
SW1A 2HQ

Or you can telephone the House of Lords Appointment Commission on 020 7271 0848.

The Standing Council of Baronetage

This body represents Baronets, and a lot of useful information, including addressing a baronet, the rules of succession, and lots more, can be found on their website:

www.baronetage.org

Appendix C: Glossary

Armigerous: A person or family that is entitled to bear a coat of arms. The Latin word *Armiger* means Arms-Bearer.

Baron: The lowest rank of the peerage, ranking below a viscount but above the non-peerage rank of baronet. The feminine form of baron is baroness.

Baronet: A hereditary title ranking below a baron, but above most knights. The exceptional knighthoods which rank above baronets are the *Most Noble Order of the Garter* and the *Most Ancient and Noble Order of the Thistle.*

Baronetess: A woman who holds a baronetcy in her own right. (Note that the wife of a Baronet is not a called a baronetess.)

Blue Blood: This term, meaning of aristocratic stock, possibly originated in Spain.

It is thought that in medieval times, while the lower classes laboured on the fields and so were tanned by the sun, European aristocrats, who spent more of their time indoors or under parasols, were paler in comparison, and their blue veins stood out against their white skin.

Coat of Arms: A unique heraldic design on a shield, given to individuals or families, usually of aristocratic or wealthy stock. Individuals can apply for arms today, but generally need to have made an exceptional contribution to society. (See Appendix B for information on the College of Arms.)

Coronet: A small crown with decorations signifying a peer's rank. It differs from a tiara in that it encircles the head whereas a tiara does not. While crowns are worn by royalty and have arches, coronets are worn by the nobility and do not have arches.

The word comes from the French *coronete* which itself is a diminutive of the word *couronne* which means crown. These words, in turn, are derived from the Latin *corona*, which means wreath.

Peers generally only wear coronets, along with their coronation robes, for a royal coronation.

Noble families are sometimes unable to afford coronets, but do have the coronet put on their coat of arms, to signify rank.

Count: The foreign equivalent of an earl. The word count does appear indirectly in the titles of the English Aristocracy, for instance the wife of an earl is titled countess, and the rank directly below an earl is viscount.

Dame: An honour conferred upon a woman by the

monarch, ranking equally with a knighthood, but below a baronet or baronetess.

Duke: The highest rank of the peerage. The feminine form is duchess.

Courtesy Title: A title given to a child of a peer (either a life peer or a hereditary peer). A child who gains a courtesy title may be a peer's child by birth or by adoption.

The title a woman might gain upon marriage to a peer, baronet or knight, is not a courtesy title.

Earl: The third highest rank of the peerage, ranking below a marquess but above a viscount. The feminine form is countess.

Ermine: A fur consisting of a white background and a pattern of black shapes, representing the winter coat of a stoat.

Heir Apparent: A person, male or female, who is first in the line of succession to a title, and who cannot be displaced by the birth of another person.

Heir Presumptive: A person, male or female, who is currently in the position to inherit a title, but whose position can be displaced by the birth of an heir apparent.

Inheritance Tax: A tax on the estate of a deceased person. Such taxes, known by any number of names including inheritance tax and death duties, have been around for centuries, with the rate of tax being raised and lowered over time.

Currently (as of 2014) only estates worth more than £325,000 are taxed, and the rate is 40%. The tax rate was higher for much of the twentieth century, and since 1900 some 1,200 stately homes have been demolished, often because owners, who inherited their properties, had to hand over a large proportion of their inheritance to the government, and were subsequently unable to pay for the upkeep of their ancestral home.

Landed Gentry: Upper class landowners, who lacked the titles of the aristocracy, but who owned enough land to live of the rental income. Most landed gentry were armigerous, and were often related to aristocratic families.

Lord of the Manor: A purchasable title, which may confer certain rights upon the holder. It is not a title that is bestowed on the holder by the Monarch and has no ranking in relation to other titles. For these reasons it is seen by some as being of little or no value.

Knight: A person granted a knighthood by the monarch for services to the country. With a couple of exceptions most knights rank below baronets. The exceptional knighthoods which rank above baronets are the *Most Noble Order of the Garter* and the *Most Ancient and Noble Order of the Thistle.*

Mantle: The mantle is a robe of crimson velvet, lined with white taffeta. It is decorated with bars of ermine, the number of bars on the robe reflecting the peer's rank.

Peers often have (or had) two mantles; one for the coronation of a monarch, which they might wear only once, and one for wearing in the House of Lords.

Marquess (or Marquis): The second highest rank of the peerage, ranking below a duke but above an earl. The feminine form is marchioness.

The Most Illustrious Order of Saint Patrick: An obsolete Irish title that ranked alongside the English *Most Noble Order of the Garter* and the Scottish *Most Ancient and Noble Order of the Thistle.* The last time this title was awarded was in 1936, and the last living recipient died in 1974. Their motto was *Quis Separabit?* (Who will separate us?)

Privy Counsellor: A member of the privy council; a body of advisors to the sovereign. Members are entitled to the style The Right Honourable.

Squire: Sometimes called a country squire, these were

men who owned a stately home and land. Squires often owned a village, and were the senior figure within village life.

Squires were also part of the landed gentry. They were sometimes related to members of the aristocracy, and had coats of arms.

A Lord of the Manor was sometimes referred to as the squire by his tenants. (See the chapter on Lords of the Manor for more information.)

Stately Home: A large house located in the countryside, and often the principal home (or "seat") of an aristocrat.

Many of these grand houses are no longer owned by the aristocracy, in part because of the free spending of one or more ancestors, but in the main because of inheritance tax. Many stately homes were demolished between the wars, and a large number of those stately homes that still exist are owned by charitable organizations such as the National Trust.

Many aristocratic families who have managed to hold on to their homes, have opened them to the public, so as to help pay for the estate. These grand homes may be open for people to visit, for instance Hatfield House in Hertfordshire, or they may be turned into elegant accommodation, for instance Askham Hall in Cumbria.

Tiara: Often used by the aristocracy to signify the

transition of a woman from the family she was born into, to her husband's family. A woman may wear her family tiara for the first time on her wedding day, and after her marriage she would wear a tiara from her husband's family. This tradition was observed by Lady Diana Spencer, who wore one of her family's tiaras when she married Prince Charles.

A tiara, unlike a coronet, does not signify rank, and may be worn by a married woman from *any* social class. Tiaras are generally worn at official banquets, receptions and dances, but for most women today, the only time they are likely to wear a tiara is on their wedding day.

Viscount: The fourth highest rank of the peerage, ranking below an earl but above a baron. The feminine form is viscountess.

Appendix D: Order of Precedence

Order of Precedence

There are separate orders of precedence for men and women, and they have been listed separately. The full order of precedence includes royalty, various government officials and others. As it is a long list, it has been edited here to only reflect the ranks of the English aristocracy.

For the sake of brevity, I have used masculine terms duke, marquess, earl, viscount, baron, baronet and knight, in places when in fact I should also have used terms such as "duchess in her own right", "marchioness in her own right" and so on. For instance, the person ranked fourth on the Male Order of Precedence is given as the "Eldest sons of non-royal dukes" whereas it should more correctly be the "Eldest sons of non-royal dukes or eldest sons of duchesses in their own right". Similarly the rank of "Wives of younger sons of barons" should really read "Wives of younger sons of barons or wives of younger sons of baronesses in their own right", and so on.

The full and current Order of Precedence, including royalty, various government officials and others, can be easily found on any number of websites.

Male Order of Precedence

Dukes
Marquesses
Eldest sons of dukes
Earls
Eldest sons of marquesses
Younger sons of dukes
Viscounts
Eldest sons of earls
Younger sons of marquesses
Barons (including life peers)
Eldest sons of viscounts
Younger sons of earls
Eldest sons of barons
Knights of the Garter and Knights of the Thistle
Younger sons of viscounts
Younger sons of Barons (not including life peers)
All sons of life peers
Baronets
Knights
Eldest sons of younger sons of peers
Eldest sons of baronets
Eldest sons of knights
Younger sons of baronets
Younger sons of knights

Female Order of Precedence

Duchesses
Marchionesses
Wives of eldest sons of dukes
Daughters of dukes not married to peers
Countesses
Wives of eldest sons of marquesses
Marquesses' daughters not married to peers
Wives of younger sons of dukes
Viscountesses
Wives of eldest sons of earls
Earls' daughters not married to peers
Wives of younger sons of marquesses
Baronesses (including life peers)
Wives of eldest sons of viscounts
Viscounts' daughters not married to peers
Wives of younger sons of earls
Wives of eldest sons of barons
Barons' daughters not married to peers
Ladies of the Garter
Ladies of the Thistle
Wives of Knights of the Garter (who are not already ranked higher)
Wives of Knights of the Thistle (who are not already ranked higher)
Wives of younger sons of viscounts

Wives of younger sons of barons
Baronetesses
Wives of baronets
Dames
Wives of Knights
Wives of the eldest sons of sons of peers
Daughters of sons of peers
Wives of the eldest sons of baronets
Daughters of baronets
Wives of the eldest sons of knights
Daughters of knights
Wives of younger sons of baronets
Wives of younger sons of knights

Appendix E: Summary of Forms of Address

Summary of Forms of Address

This section gives a simplified recap of the forms of address mentioned earlier in the book.

The examples in this section, such as the Duke of Buckminster, are fictional examples.

This section gives only general rules which occasionally have exceptions. For a more detailed account on addressing the English aristocracy, please refer back to the relevant chapters.

Forms of Address for Dukes

Envelope

(His Grace) The Duke of Buckminster

Beginning of a letter

My Lord Duke
or
Dear Duke

In person

Your Grace
or
Duke

Forms of Address for Duchesses

Envelope

(Her Grace) The Duchess of Buckminster

Beginning of a letter

Madam

or

Dear Duchess

In person

Your Grace

or

Duchess

Forms of Address for Marquesses

Envelope

(The Most Honourable) the Marquesss of Stockbridge

Beginning of a letter

My Lord Marquess
or
Dear Lord Stockbridge

In person

My lord
or
Your lordship
or
Lord Stockbridge

Forms of Address for Marchionesses

Envelope

(The Most Honourable) the Marchioness of
Stockbridge

Beginning of a letter

Madam
or
Dear Lady Stockbridge

In person

My lady
or
Your ladyship
or
Lady Stockbridge

Forms of Address for Earls

Envelope

(The Right Honourable) the Earl of Menai

Beginning of a letter

My Lord
or
Dear Lord Menai

In person

My lord
or
Your lordship
or
Lord Menai

Forms of Address for Countesses

Envelope

(The Right Honourable) the Countess of Menai

Beginning of a letter

Madam

or

Lady Menai

In person

My Lady

or

Your Ladyship

or

Lady Menai

Forms of Address for Viscounts

Envelope

(The Right Honourable) the Viscount Haversham

Beginning of a letter

My lord
or
Dear Lord Haversham

In person

My lord
or
Your lordship
or
Lord Haversham

Forms of Address for Viscountesses

Envelope

(The Right Honourable) Viscountess Haversham

Beginning of a letter

Madam
or
Dear Lady Haversham

In person

My lady
or
Your ladyship
or
Lady Haversham

Forms of Address for Barons

Envelope

(The Right Honourable) the Lord Vaynol

Beginning of a letter

My Lord
or
Dear Lord Vaynol

In person

My lord
or
Your lordship
or
Lord Vaynol

Forms of Address for Baronesses

Envelope

(The Right Honourable) the Lady Vaynol

Beginning of a letter

Madam
or
Dear Lady Vaynol

In person

Your ladyship
or
Lady Vaynol

Forms of Address for Baronets

Envelope

Sir John Smith, Bt

Beginning of a letter

Sir

or

Dear Sir John

or

Dear Sir John Smith

In person

Sir

or

Sir John

Forms of Address for the Wives of Baronets

Envelope

Lady Smith

Beginning of a letter

Madam

or

Dear Lady Smith

In person

My lady

or

Lady Smith

Forms of Address for Knights

Envelope

Sir John Smith

Beginning of a letter

Sir
or
Dear Sir John

In person

Sir
or
Sir John

Forms of Address for the Wives of Knights

Envelope

Lady Smith

Beginning of a letter

Madam
or
Dear Lady Smith

In person

My lady
or
Lady Smith

Forms of Address for Dames

Envelope

Dame Jane Smith

Beginning of a letter

Madam

or

Dear Dame Jane

or

Dear Jane Smith

In person

Madam

or

Dame Jane

Appendix F: Servants

Servants

Today very few households employ large numbers of servants, but at the beginning of the twentieth century, according to the United Kingdom's 1911 census, there were around 1.3 million people working n domestic service, outnumbering the 1.2 million people who worked in agriculture and the 1 million coal miners. Most of these servants were not employed in grand households but by large numbers middle class workers such as lawyers and doctors.

In the grandest houses there could be over a hundred servants who worked to a hierarchy as strict as any upstairs with the butler and housekeeper at the top and the likes of scullery maids, who scrubbed the pots and pans, and boot boys who would spend their days polishing the shoes and boots of their masters, at the bottom.

On social occasions when the owner of a large estate invited a number of aristocrats to their home, valets and lady's maids from other estates would accompany their masters and mistresses. Upstairs, the aristocrats would be seated for dinner in a strict order of precedence. Downstairs, valets and lady's maids would be known, not by their own names but by the names of their masters and mistresses, and at meal times would be seated according to the rank of their employer, so reflecting the seating arrangement upstairs.

With the general demise of grand houses, and also with the advent of technological innovations such as the washing machine, dish washer, vacuum cleaner and so on, there are far fewer people employed in domestic service today than at the beginning of the twentieth century.

Servants had a wide variety of roles and duties, and their job-titles often reflected the duties they undertook. The most common roles have been included in the following list.

In Victorian and Edwardian stately homes the approximate rank of servants was as follows:

Butler

The highest ranking servant, in charge of male staff. His work also involved looking after the wine, and, along with the footmen, serving meals at the family table.

Butlers ranked below Estate Managers, who were employed to run the estate as a whole and were not considered to be servants. Estate managers, however, would rarely get involved in servant matters.

The title of butler comes from the Old French *botellier* which was the name given to the person who looked after the king's wine.

Today there are some female butlers, but this is a recent development, and most households who employ butlers, particularly overseas, tend to prefer male butlers.

As there are fewer stately homes operating with large amounts of servants, the modern butler may take on other roles such as chauffeur or valet as and when needed.

Housekeeper

The highest ranking female servant, in charge of female staff. She was paid slightly less than the butler, and as well as managing staff, she would ensure the furnishings were well maintained.

As with modern-day butlers, housekeepers today may find themselves carrying out a wide range of duties that, in Victorian and Edwardian times, they might have delegated to more junior servants.

Cook

The cook, as well as preparing meals for her employers, was in charge of kitchen staff including assistant cooks and scullery maids.

A good cook was much sought after by the aristocracy, and they were sometimes imported from other countries. Such was the demand for the very best cooks that they were often enticed with good wages, and could occasionally earn more than the butler.

Valet

A valet was, and is, a male servant who assisted the master of the house, and generally did not undertake any duties other than those given by the master.

A valet would help look after the master's clothes, run his master's bath, and would sometimes undertake secretarial work. Valets were usually employed by the master directly, rather than through the butler.

The word valet can be pronounced without the "t", rhyming with ballet, or it can be pronounced with the "t", rhyming with mallet.

Valets were sometimes known as a "gentleman's gentleman".

Lady's Maid

A lady's maid was a private servant who assisted the mistress of the house. Lady's maids would also act as companions as well as servants, because they would often spend much of their time in their mistress's company. A lady's maid's daily duties might involve altering garments, and styling her mistress's hair.

A lady's maid was of a similar rank to a valet.

Footman

In larger households there would be a number of footmen, the highest ranking of whom was called first footman. One of their main duties was to serve food at the family's table. Like parlour maids, another of their jobs was to answer the door and welcome guests. Some footmen would go on to become valets or butlers.

Traditionally only men waited at the family table, namely valets and the butler, this began to change during the First World War when most young men were away fighting and there was a shortage of men in service. During the war, female servants took on many traditional male roles, such as serving food, and often continued to do so, even after the war ended.

Nanny

Nannies (also known as nurses) looked after babies and young children, and were sometimes assisted by nursery maids (also called nursemaids).

Many aristocratic children became very fond of their nannies, and often the relationship was more like that of a mother and child, not least when the child's actual mother and father were regularly absent, or took little interest in their child.

Nannies would often work for the same family for many years, helping to raise generations of children.

Chamber Maid

A chamber maid's main duty would be to clean and maintain the bedrooms. She would also ensure fires were lit, and she would bring hot water upstairs for baths.

Parlour Maid

A parlour maid's main duty would be to clean and

maintain the rooms downstairs. She would also serve afternoon tea, and sometimes, like footmen, she would answer the door and welcome guests.

Housemaid

A housemaid would have more general duties, usually cleaning any part of the house that needed attending to, and helping out where necessary, under the guidance of more senior servants, not least the housekeeper.

Kitchen Maid

Kitchen maids assisted with kitchen chores. Sometimes there would be a hundred and more guests upstairs, so there would be the need for any number of kitchen maids to help prepare elaborate dishes. A good kitchen maid could go on to become an assistant cook, and then a highly-paid cook.

Scullery Maid

One of the lowest ranking servants, the scullery maid was usually one of the youngest servants, and one of the lowest paid. She would spend hours scrubbing pots and pans, scouring the kitchen floor, and so on.

In the middle ages, when female servants were rare, there were male equivalents of scullery maids called scullions.

Hall Boy

A low ranking male servant, the hall boy, would carry out some of the most menial and unpleasant tasks, such as emptying chamber pots. He was roughly the same rank as a scullery maid.

Boot Boy

A boot boy, or boots as they were sometimes called, was usually a teenager or young boy whose job was to clean the household members' shoes or boots. He would sometimes also act as hall boy. He was the lowest ranking male servant.

There were also a number of outdoor servants who were not part of the household hierarchy. On a large estate these servants might include:

Head Gardener

The head gardener was in charge of maintaining the grounds of the estate, and could preside over dozens of workers who maintained the grounds. On large estates there were often more gardeners than household servants.

Game Keeper

The game keeper ensured there was enough game for shooting, and also maintained the woods, rivers and so on for the benefit of the wildlife. He would also try to prevent any poaching of animals, and might come into conflict with both trespassers and poachers.

Coachman

The coachman's role was to drive a horse-drawn carriage and escort the family of the house. The role of coachman was largely superseded by the role of the chauffeur. On smaller estates, the coachman would also act as groom or stable master.

Stable Master

The stable master was in charge of stables and horses, and would be in charge of any grooms.

Groom

The groom would spend his days tending to the horses, ensuring they were well fed, well watered and in good health. The groom would also maintain riding equipment.

Chauffeur

The chauffeur took over the role of driving the members of their employer's family from the coachman, in the early years of the twentieth century. Today, now that most people can drive, the butler or valet may, in addition to their traditional tasks, be given the task of acting as chauffeur.

In the early days of chauffeuring, and to a lesser extent, today, the chauffeur would have a good working knowledge of the car he drove, and would be able to fix many of the car's mechanical problems himself.

In addition to servants, there were other employees on grand estates who were not seen as servants, and these people were largely drawn from the middle-classes. These included:

Governess

The governess's role of educating the children of her master and mistress is well-known. It was usually, though not always, girls who were educated by the governess, as the boys tended to be sent off to boarding school. The children would often be taught French or another language, the piano or another instrument, as well as painting, poetry and other genteel activities.

Well-educated middle class women who had not married, and needed an income, had a limited number of jobs available to them that they might consider proper. Sometimes prospective governesses came from quite well-to-do backgrounds, but had fallen on hard times, perhaps with the death or bankruptcy of their father, and so had to go out and work for a living.

The position of governess was often a lonely one, being neither a member of the family, nor a household servant. She would often find herself in social limbo, between the upper class family and the lower class servants, neither of whom saw her as one of their own. As a result she would usually eat alone, and have little social contact with other adults.

If she was attractive, or even if she was not, the mistress of the house could sometimes perceive the governess as a threat (real or imagined) to the mistress's marriage, and there would often be tensions as a result.

The governess might, on occasions, preside over the nanny (or nurse), and nursery maids.

A governess, being from a middle-class or even an upper-middle class background, might well have been brought up in a household where servants were employed by her family, and she would not see her role of governess as a servant role.

Governesses were not part of the household system of servants, and did not answer to the housekeeper or butler, but in reality, her subservient role was not as different to the role of servants as she might like to admit.

Not surprisingly, given their unusual and often unhappy positions, governesses were common characters in fiction in the late nineteenth and early twentieth centuries (for example, the unnamed governess in *The Turn of the Screw,* by Henry James, or Violet Hunter in the Sherlock Holmes tale *The Adventure of the Copper Beeches* by Sir Arthur Conan Doyle).

Lady's Companion

Aristocratic women, or women of wealth, sometimes employed women of genteel birth to act as their companions. Lady's companions were, like governesses, usually drawn from middle class women who were in need of a respectable income. A lady's companion was not seen as a servant, and provided companionship and assistance. She would be given a room upstairs with the family, rather than in the servants' quarters, and would not be expected to do any of the servants' work such as cleaning or cooking. Instead, as well as acting as a companion, she would assist her companion in a variety of ways, such as entertaining guests, and attending social functions with her employer.

If the aristocratic employer was a young woman, then her companion might act as a chaperone, in the days when it was seen as improper for an upper class woman to receive a man, who was not her relative, alone.

The position of lady's companion had similarities to the lower ranking position of lady's maid.

There is a cultural example of a lady's companion, in the television series *Upstairs, Downstairs*. In the episode *An Object of Value* there is the rather snobbish Miss Hodges, who was the companion to an elderly dowager Countess.

Estate Manager

The estate manager was not a servant, but an employee, usually well-educated, who ran the estate as a whole.

He would often report to the owner of the estate, about the buying and selling of land, crop yields, the building of houses and farm buildings, and so on. He would also liaise with lawyers, accountants, architects and other professionals, as well as tenants.

The estate manager was usually the best-paid employee on the estate.

As his role could be large and time-consuming he would sometimes have help, usually in the form of a deputy estate manager.

Printed in Great Britain
by Amazon

67363158R00119